Inherently Fallible

Life Lessons From A Father

Written by Shawn Janes

Edited by Stacy Padula

Briley & Baxter Publications | Plymouth, Massachusetts

ISBN: 978-1-954819-06-1

Book Design: Stacy O'Halloran

For Ansley and Ben.
You are all that is best in me.

Preface

Do you have something to say or just want to say something? I'm not one to ramble or mince words, and hopefully, neither is this book, so I'll keep it short and to the point. Your time is valuable, and if you're at all like me when it comes to reading, there is nothing quite as frustrating as a 300-page book that could have been condensed to 30 pages. You may find that some of these topics are short and abruptly come to an end. That's the intention.

I believe I have something to say, and although I'm an expert and master of nothing, I have experience in many things. That may sound and appear like a recipe for a well-rounded person, but it's actually a hazardous combination of a short attention span and lack of patience. This has resulted in a lot of mistakes and some achievements, throughout the years. A life lived looking over my shoulder as the past seems to be one step behind me, waiting for that slight pause or misstep so it can pounce and unleash its predetermined fury on my life—an inherited fallibility constantly in my shadow. My mother didn't escape it, neither did my brother, and time will only tell if I will either, but I have learned a few things throughout the years. Some critical life lessons that should be passed on to my children and the children of others. I hope this will help you avoid some of the mistakes I have made and find success where I have failed. My desire is not that you have a pain free life. I believe pain is an unfortunate necessity of life and the ultimate teacher for our development and change. Still, some problems could have been simply avoided by the insight and experience of others. May this help you on your adventure of life; it's an ass-kicker.

*"It's not that I'm smart;
it's that I stay with a problem longer."*
- Albert Einstein

Effort > Outcome = Ready

I've always felt like I have to work harder than other people to reach a goal. You know those kids in school who partied every night, rarely studied, and got straight "A's"? I never liked them. Rarely in life did things seem to come at a leisurely, smooth pace. I discovered an unpleasant truth about success while I was preparing to give a speech. It is probably something you and I have always known subconsciously but have never been taught. For me, it became clear when I had reached a point in my preparation where I felt like the effort I was putting into this project had exceeded the value of the desired result. I realized that once I had put more effort into this speech than what it was arguably worth, it was probably ready. For the first time I could remember, I crossed this imaginary line where the preparation exceeded the results. This is also the point when you have worked so hard at something that you start asking yourself whether it is worth the effort? But the truth is that crossing this line leads to success in almost anything you want to achieve and solidifies any question about its value and importance to you. I believe people who have achieved some of the most significant accomplishments in life fully understand this rule.

I recently watched one of the most amazing human physical achievements of all time. In the awarding-winning documentary, *Free Solo*, Alex Honnold climbed one of the most iconic rock formations on the earth. A 3,000-foot granite wall in Yosemite National Park called El Capitan. The most remarkable part of this climb was that he did it without a rope. I was captivated and inspired by his meticulous preparation. Alex obsessed over the placement of his hands and feet every step of the way. Every twist, turn, step, and hold, was meticulously noted in a journal for this 3,000-foot climb. He knew that if he got one of those wrong, it was all over. While most of us don't deal with these types of consequences, we should still be just as willing to put in the groundwork if we want to achieve success. We witness the achievements of others with no knowledge of how they made it to that point. We rarely get a glimpse of the discipline, the struggle, pain, or the sacrifices that our heroes endure to meet their goals. It's easy to witness the end result and say, "I want that." It's another thing to immerse yourself into something so deeply that the effort you put in is greater than the worth of the outcome. When you cross this line, you are onto something.

"He that can have patience can have what he will."
- Benjamin Franklin

Almost every mistake I have ever made was a result of my impatience or need for instant gratification. Let me repeat that: almost... every... mistake. Looking back, had I waited, had I first sought advice, had I possessed an ounce of patience, I could have avoided some painful situations. I would be in a better position today. I would be a different person today. Outside of love, patience could be the most important personal virtue. There are few circumstances or situations in life that don't require some degree of patience. While there are times when we need to move quickly without thinking or waiting, those are few and far between. As we all know, waiting is difficult and, at times, can be excruciating. It's that narrow road that Frost wrote about—the difficult choice. For those who can wait, it leads to a more satisfied and fulfilled life.

A little bit every day. The turtle beats the rabbit.

I'll admit, in the story of the rabbit and the turtle, I'm more like the rabbit. I have experience running myself into exhaustion in what looks like hyper-production and accomplishment. Rabbits look good from the surface and often project the appearance of success under the essence of busyness, but they are also the ones who are burning out and combusting internally. We go through certain times in our lives when it feels like a sprint is necessary, but as John Firth said, if you keep your nose to the grindstone too long, you'll end up with a disfigured face.

On the other hand, the turtle was slow but consistent and steady, which is why she had the confidence to challenge the rabbit to the race and ultimately win. This enduring commitment will almost always result in success. With that wisdom, you can ask yourself, *What is important to you? Do you need to get or stay in shape?* It doesn't have to be an intense regimen that leads to exhaustion. Even a simple workout routine can do wonders over time with dedication. Have you always wanted to start writing or journaling? I was able to write this short book, one turtle step at a time—sometimes as little as a word or sentence a day. Small, consistent steps every day will always bring you to the finish line. Whereas "I'll try," "I need to," or "I should" people, will never make it. Like Yoda said, "Do or do not. There is no try." Surely you have heard those stories of people who were paralyzed or in a tragic accident. Told they would never walk again, forever confined to a wheelchair, they defied the doctor's prognosis and made consistent efforts and small steps every day until they learned to walk again or even run again. Consistency and commitment win.

"Money, so they say..."
- Pink Floyd

I've probably heard the song "Money" by Pink Floyd a hundred times on the radio, but I've never listened to the lyrics. It's a catchy tune with a powerful message. If you're a fan, try listening to the song and pay attention to the lyrics. It takes on a whole new meaning.

There are two things parents rarely talk to their children about: money and sex. They weren't talking points in my house. When it came to money, the underlying message was to get and earn as much as you can. It may not have looked like it from the outside, but with a single mom raising two boys, we lived mostly week to week, hand to mouth. Money was about survival. The more you had, the better you survived. There was no talk of savings, investments, IRA's, 401k's, or retirement. That was way too far in the future. We were thinking about next week, not next year.

There are so many things I could say about money. The pain, abuse, mismanagement, greed, etc., and this is just in my own life. My simple advice here would be this, be generous with what you have and save for the future. I have always considered myself a generous person. Giving is not something I have to work at or consciously think about, like sharing my feelings. It's just been a part of me. Generosity always felt natural. I, like most of us, enjoy helping people. The danger with charity, and what I have had to be mindful of, are my motives. If I am giving to make myself feel better or because I believe there was some form of good karma for me in this action, then my generosity is in trouble. The litmus test for generosity is whether you are willing to give to others without being acknowledged or even recognized for your contribution.

Savings is a whole other issue. I have no gifting or instincts in that aspect. When you are in your 20's the last thing on your mind is what retirement will look like. When you are in your 50's all you think about is, "why didn't I take this seriously in my 20's?" We are easily fooled when it comes to money. Consider this, if you were offered a job for $100,000 a year in annual income, how do you see that salary? Do you now have $100,000 to spend on your needs and desires? Should you buy your house and set up your lifestyle based on $100,000? Some see this as a six-figure $100,000 income; others know they will need to set aside at least 30% for Federal and State taxes, Social Security, and Medicare. In addition, 10% should go to savings for your emergency or rainy-day fund. Another 10% will be applied to a retirement fund. After all of that, your big $100,000 salary just transformed to $50,000. The problem is that most people don't save the 10% for retirement or the 10% for an emergency, and they live on the $70,000 but think they have $100,000. Be realistic in what you have and earn. Start putting money away early. Money that cannot be easily accessed. Cultivating a little self-denial and discipline now will pay dividends and compounded interest with more than just finances in the future.

*"Character consists of what you do
on the third and fourth tries."*
- James Michener

Many people allow an inevitable barrier to end their quest: the first "no." A rejection. That little voice telling you to stop. This is where the average person gives up, unaware that failure is a part of the process. The truth is, you will probably fail and be rejected far more than you succeed. It's part of our development and one most people don't understand.

What does the failure rate look like on the road to success? JK Rowling was penniless and living on welfare while twelve major publishers rejected her Harry Potter book. Colonel Sanders was sixty-five years old, and he was turned down 1,009 times before his famous chicken recipe was accepted once. Kathryn Stockett's book, *The Help*, was rejected by sixty literary agents. Can you imagine sixty rejections and continuing to believe in your product? No way I would have pushed through sixty people telling me "no." If you want something bad enough and you believe in it, keep working at it. Keep moving when others quit. I love the quote from Lone Survivor that says, "Anything worth doing is worth overdoing; mediocrity is for cowards." Persistence is key.

On my way to work one day, I got to the office and realized I didn't have my wallet. Backtracking my steps, I traced its last known location to the gas pump where I had filled up my car. I immediately went back to the gas station, which was connected to a grocery store, and searched for the wallet. I didn't see it, so I asked the attendant if anyone had turned in a wallet. All I received was a quick "no" from the disinterested employee, but I was determined and continued pressing on. For some reason, I didn't believe my wallet had been stolen, so I went inside the grocery store and asked the help desk if they had found a wallet.

"Not that I remember," was the reply.

"Do you have a lost and found area?" I asked.

"Yes, but the manager is the only one with access."

"Could you call the manager, please?"

The manager showed up, and I asked him the same question. He said he didn't recall anyone turning in a wallet, so I asked if he could check the lost and found. He went into the room and came back with what in his hand? My wallet. Someone had seen it sitting on top of the gas pump and turned it into one of the employees who put it in the lost and found area. Now, where would you have given up on your search for the wallet? Most days, I would have quit right away, but the thought of canceling credit cards and getting a new license motivated me to explore every option. Persistence is a valuable trait, but it doesn't always lead to success. I have persistently dug myself deeper and deeper into bad situations, but it still teaches me something about myself along the way. Many things can seem impossible until they are finished.

"Advice seeks to help, not to please."
- Shawn Janes

Don't seek counsel from someone who can't help you. Why would I seek advice from someone who can't help me? Because I can always find someone who will agree with me and tell me what I *want* to hear instead of what I *need* to hear. A true friend gives it to you straight. They don't always agree with you, and they aren't afraid to tell you the hard truth. These are people you respect and admire, preferably someone who has had some experience in the area you are seeking help. You wouldn't seek financial advice from someone who is broke, nor would you plan a fitness regimen with someone who is unhealthy. Everyone has an opinion, and most are quick to give it to you. Beware of the pleasers. They will align with your opinion regardless of the truth. We all desire friends who stay with us through any trial, but a true friend isn't afraid to hurt your feelings and is willing to risk the relationship to ensure you are on the right path.

"Find a group of people who challenge and inspire you;
spend a lot of time with them,
and it will change your life."
- Amy Poehler

Surround yourself with people you want to resemble. Look around at your friends right now, and you will see your future. The people you spend time with will reveal the condition of your soul and the direction of your life. Do they build you up or bring you down? Be careful: just because people accept you as you are doesn't mean they are the right relationships for you. Good friends call you out, challenge you, hold you accountable, and are usually doing the things you want to do.
A healthy balance of friends might exist in three groups.

1. Friends you are leading and have influence over. These are people who want to be where you are. The ones your pour into, develop, and teach.

2. Friends with whom you have the most in common. They are intellectual equals, and the ones most aligned with you. You probably spend most of your time with these relationships.
3. Friends who influence your life. These are the people you aspire to emulate. They have reached the places in life you want to achieve. They might be the whole package or just winning in an area of life where you want to succeed. It's essential that you don't just know these people, but they know you.

Your real friendships will be the ones that stay close to you when tragedy strikes. When you make a colossal mistake or poor decision. This is a great way to test and see if the people in your life are authentic. Do something stupid and take inventory of who remains by your side and who steps back and is waiting for you to get your shit together. Your true friends are the people who stay with you no matter what. It may surprise you to find out how few there are.

*"It's easy to stand with the crowd.
It takes courage to stand alone."
- Mahatma Gandhi*

The world can be a lonely and isolating place sometimes. Sticking to your beliefs and making the right choices will often come at a price. There will be times when you will find yourself standing all alone while the crowd moves on. Stay true to what you believe. Sacrifices made now will be rewarded later. To get to the places you have never been, you may have to make choices that others choose to avoid. Outliers are often the ones who bring the change needed in the world, themselves, and others.

"My life has been filled with terrible misfortune,
most of which has never happened."
- Michel de Montaigne

I do an excellent job of hiding the anxiety that I carry. I will often find myself consumed by "what if" scenarios. Most of these concerns are insignificant and have a low probability of ever becoming a reality. You know what I'm talking about. What if I don't find a job? What if I lose my job? What if this doesn't work out? What if I can't make that payment? What if the test results are positive? What if I made the wrong decision? And on and on they go. I will never forget leaving work one day, stressed out to the max while "what if" questions ran through my mind. As I approached the elevator, I pulled the keys out of my pocket, aimed my car remote at the elevator, and pushed the unlock button. I quickly checked my phone for emails assuming the elevator was busy. After a couple of minutes, I started to think the elevator might be broken. I reached in my pocket again, grabbed my keys, and aimed it at the elevator expecting a new result. I looked at the elevator buttons to see none of them were lit up and quickly realized what was happening. That's what stress can do to your mind. I would have enjoyed seeing that episode on the security camera.

Researchers at Penn State University did a study about the things people worry about and discovered that 91% of the possible scenarios that consume our minds would never actually happen. Some of the participants in the study found that none of the things they worried about actually happened. This data probably won't convince you to stop worrying; I still do, but there is an exercise I use that helps with my own anxiety. While attending a training session about the impact of stress on the body, the instructor recommended a simple practice that has proven to be effective when those "what if" scenarios start running through your head. She challenged us to focus on the situation we were concerned about and mentally walk through the worst-case scenario. What is the worst possible outcome, and how will it impact me? Going through this simple exercise can help alleviate those "what if" concerns. You might find out that even the worst-case scenario isn't as bad as you thought. What if I can't find a job? I might have to move back in with my parents. Not the outcome I was looking for, but my mom is a great cook, and I haven't seen my parents in a while. However, sometimes it is what it is. Maybe they don't survive that disease. What will life look like if that happens? Walk your mind through the things that keep you up at night, and you might find a less frantic you on the other end.

*"Most people never ask, and that's what separates,
sometimes, the people who do things from
the people who just dream about them."*
- Steve Jobs

When Steve Jobs was twelve years old, he wanted to build a frequency counter—yeah, I don't know what that is either, but he didn't have the parts he needed. He decided to look up Bill Hewlett's phone number in the phone book and give him a call. Bill is the founder of Hewlett Packard, which was at one time the largest computer company in the world. To Steve's surprise, Bill answered the phone himself. Steve explained what he was doing and asked Bill if he had any spare parts to build a frequency counter. Bill not only got Steve the parts he needed for his frequency counter, but also offered Steve a job that summer at Hewlett Packard.

I've heard the "you have not because you ask not" reference many times, and it sounds good, but I didn't put much belief in it until I actually started asking. When I say "asking," I mean asking for things that were wildly out of my comfort zone. One of the first businesses I was ever involved in was a utility consulting company that a friend and I started. We were a two-person operation trying to start a business while maintaining full-time jobs. Since we were a new operation, we focused our efforts on working with smaller companies that would be less interested in our brief history. Things were moving slow, so I decided to take a leap and try to get in front of some larger organizations. I started with one of the most prominent companies in the area, American Express. I made a few phone calls, and to my surprise, they agreed to meet with us. I'll admit there was a part of me that didn't expect to get a meeting with American Express. I was nervous but went into this meeting with the confidence that I had more knowledge about the subject than they did. The meeting went well, and they became our largest and most profitable client. Clearly, that plan didn't work for every prospect, but it did give me the courage to keep asking. Try starting at the very top of your expectations or wildest dreams, and you might be shocked at the access you get by just asking.

I'm sure Steve Jobs would have been a success without the influence and help from Bill Hewlett, but he shares that experience as one that deeply impacted him. I routinely observe people who settle for and accept what they have been offered, or believe they should have, instead of asking for what they want. I'd be willing to bet you know someone who has exceptional potential but settled for what they could find instead of what they were capable of doing. Two excuses usually exist—unbelief in themselves or a history of failure from when they did try.

You've got nothing to lose and everything to gain. If you don't ask, the answer will always be "no."

"Leave it better than you found it."
- Robert Baden-Powell

I have two things neighbors and friends like to borrow: my tools and my truck. I don't mind lending anything I have as long as the item is returned in the same condition as when it left. Trucks are handy when you have something large to move or need to make a trip to the hardware store. I let a friend use mine to hall some mulch for their yard. When I got it back, it was dirty and nearly out of gas. Another friend needed it to move some furniture. When he returned the truck, it was washed and filled with gas. Who do you think I'd be more inclined to loan my vehicle to next time? There's a camping quote that says, "leave no trace." Meaning, let no one know you were there. Don't leave anything behind but leave everything just as you found it. The same goes for staying at someone's home, borrowing things from other people, or anything that doesn't belong to you. Honor what someone has entrusted you with, and instead of giving it back as you received it, try to make it better. Exceed their expectations.

"What goes in must come out."
- Shawn Janes

The heart and mind are pliable. You are continually processing and absorbing things every day. Some of those things are by choice, and others are not. We have some control over the things we watch, the places we go, and the people we spend time with, but there are the occasional "Jack in the Boxes" that pop up in our lives without warning—those things that catch you off guard. The words or actions of others or something that appeared on your screen that you weren't expecting. Whether we were looking for it or are victims of circumstance, the things that we absorb will eventually come out and reveal themselves in ways we can't always control. These seeds grow and shape who you are and how you act. I still have images seared in my mind that will likely never go away. It's hard to delete those from your internal hard drive. When I was young, I saw the movie *The Exorcist*, and I don't ever want to see it again. It scared me as a kid, and I still remember it today. Likewise, I will never forget the words from a friend that gave me great inspiration and hope. On the other side, I still struggle with the words that inflicted pain and doubt. Whether by choice or unsolicited, the things we see and hear will determine how we talk and act, how we treat others, and how we are seen and known. Nothing is just buried in some remote area and forgotten forever. Everything you take in is going to expose itself. The point is this: protect your mind and heart. Control what you can. The things you have allowed in will come out; whether it comes out your ass or mouth isn't always under your control.

"The world will not be destroyed by those who do evil,
but those who watch them without doing anything."
- Albert Einstein

We see and hear the stories of leaders at the highest levels failing and making poor moral choices almost daily. Never assume that people in authority or leadership are immune to mistakes or poor decisions. Be vigilant and aware of the people who are leading you—those you are following. Great leaders should be challenged and open to questions. Following someone without question or accountability is how cults are born. Have you ever wondered where the saying "don't drink the Kool-Aid" was originated? People, in general, are sheep. You may not want to hear that, but it's true. Most people want to be cared for and look for leaders to provide guidance and answers.

We need to be cautious of who we put on a pedestal. As a Veteran, I have had leaders whom I respected so much that I would have done anything for them—even given my life if they had asked. I have also served under some highly dysfunctional people who had no business leading anyone. It wasn't until I read Donald Miller's book, *Scary Close*, that I had a better understanding of how we end up with so many defective people in leadership roles. It was this question that leaped off the page and got my attention about leaders: *"What if some of the most successful people in the world got that way because their success was fueled by a misappropriated need for love?" What if the people we consider to be great are actually the most broken? And what if the whole time they're seeking applause, they are missing out on true intimacy because they've never learned how to receive it?"* I believe this resonated with me because it revealed something of myself as a leader. It also explains a lot when you look at some of the people in leadership today or in the past. Don't be afraid to ask questions. There are a lot of people who didn't and should have.

"Let no man pull you low enough to hate him."
- Martin Luther King Jr.

The Necessity Of Forgiveness

I think Foreigner said it best, "In my life, there's been heartache and pain, I don't know if I can face it again." No one escapes this life without their fair share of heartache and pain. I certainly haven't. There has been, what feels like, more than enough pain in my life. Wounds that I am not willing to write about and most that occurred as a child or young man. It had burrowed deep within me to places that couldn't be seen or repaired. I held on to this pain and my anger for the people who were responsible for a long time, probably too long. Forgiveness was not an option if you were the source of pain in my life. I wasn't going to let you off that easy. There was a price to pay. A debt that was due and five Our Fathers and ten Hail Mary's wasn't going to absolve your actions (shameless Catholic upbringing reference). I was going to collect one way or another. It took a while to finally realize I was not just a prisoner of my past; I was the warden and the judge. Overcoming my inability to let go and forgive was eventually found to be the keys to my freedom.

While working on a project, I came across a surname. It was a rare last name. It was not one you see often, but it was clear because it was my adopted name. One that had been changed for me later in life. As soon as I saw it, I knew I was still carrying the unresolved pain of this relationship, and it was my responsibility to forgive and let this go. Let me be clear; my forgiveness was not an invitation to reunite or bring them back into my life nor was it saying that what happened was okay. It was giving up the power they still had over me and letting go. It was realizing they were also a product of their environment and upbringing. So many of us are trapped in our own constructed prisons of anger, hatred, and resentment, unaware that forgiveness is the key that opens the door to our freedom. Remember that song every child in the world was singing in 2013? Well, Elsa was wrong when she said, "I'm never going back; the past is in the past. Let it go." You will have to go back to move forward. It's a vulnerable and scary step, but powerful and necessary for our growth.

"Change before you have to."
- Jack Welch

There is a universal truth about internal change: even if you understand what it is, it is unlikely you can do anything to avoid it. We are hedonistic people by nature, almost always engaged in the pursuit of pleasure and the avoidance of pain. This indulgence can often lead us to places of regret and discomfort. When we are unhappy or end up in a place we didn't expect to be, there is only one way we can, and will, escape. What is it?

When the fear of making the changes needed in our life exceeds the pain to do something different, that's when most of us will make a change. Surprisingly, most people know what is wrong and what they need to change, but they simply can't or won't do it. That is, until the pain of their situation has become more significant than the effort it will take to make a change and do something about it. Once our current situation becomes so unbearable that the change becomes the more comfortable choice, change often occurs. I'm telling you this for two reasons: first, so you can recognize it in yourself and hopefully accelerate the process; second, so you can recognize it in other people and become more sympathetic in understanding the human condition. When I see someone hurting or struggling, my instinct is to help or fix the problem. This desire or need to improve or help the situation is the unfortunate instinct and condition of most people, but I would say it's most prevalent in men. My default when I'm listening is to start working solutions in my head instead of just listening. Women seem to be designed and wired as better listeners.

Unfortunately, most people are not comfortable allowing someone to hit bottom, even when they know it is the only way to do something different and make the necessary changes in their lives. There's a song called "Cruel to Be Kind." Do you remember it? *You gotta be, cruel to be kind, in the right measure. Cruel to be kind, it's a very good sign. Cruel to be kind, means that I love you.* Now I've got this song stuck in your head all day. Nick Lowe found the inspiration to write this song from Shakespeare's *Hamlet.* In this scene, Hamlet was telling his mother, *I must be cruel only to be kind, thus the bad begins and worse remains behind.* We leave the worst behind, but it will be painful going forward. Take a quick look back on your own life and see if you can remember when you made a significant change. Your health, job, relationships. You didn't change those things until you got sick and tired of being sick and tired. This is the first step. It comes before inspiration and motivation. You weren't inspired by the commercial you saw with that healthy person on the fitness bike. You were frustrated with how you felt. The fact that your jeans were too tight. That job you hated and stayed in too long. That relationship you should have exited long ago. You didn't do something about it until the answer became easier than the situation.

I had a friend who traded his car in for a motorcycle. He was determined to ride a motorcycle everywhere. Rain, snow, cold—whatever. I tried introducing simple solutions and logic into our conversations about why he could have a motorcycle *and* a car. Why not have options to avoid the misery of inclement weather on a motorcycle every day? He wasn't following any of my unsolicited advice. A few years later, he traded in his motorcycle for a car, and I couldn't wait to ask why. "So, what happened?" I asked. "Why did you decide to get a car?" He said he was finally tired of freezing in the winter, arriving at work soaking wet, and the complete inconvenience and stupidity of it all. *Seriously?* This is precisely what I had been telling him all along, but he had to experience it himself.

If you pay attention, you will see this playing out everywhere you look, as so many people do the same thing over and over, expecting a different result. I think that might be the definition of insanity. When you understand this truth, it will help you become more sensitive and patient with people, as this process must run its course for them to be empowered in their own lives. Sometimes we have to allow the pain to exist. Trying to stop the pain or alleviating it too soon can often prolong the process.

"Your real life begins after putting your house in order."
- Marie Kondo

When I was young, I used to watch Sanford and Son. Fred Sanford was a junk dealer who would fake a heart attack in almost every episode. I might be dating myself, but the show was hilarious. What amazed me about Fred's home was the amount of junk that was scattered everywhere. Inside and out. Now mama always said, "don't judge a book by its cover," but sometimes, more than not, the cover reveals the book. How you treat yourself and your possessions will relate directly to how people treat and act around you. You don't care about your home, your body, your stuff? You can bet no one else will either. And vice versa. If you visit someone's house, and it looks like Sanford and Son, you will more than likely adapt to your surroundings and disrespect that environment based on what you see. You aren't thinking about taking off your shoes; *heck, let me throw my feet up on the coffee table!* Then there are the homes that are just the opposite, the ones where you find yourself unconsciously wiping down the sink in the bathroom when you're finished.

You don't need to have money or wealth to take care of the things you have. Wealth isn't a prerequisite for gratitude. We instinctively care for what matters to us and the things we are grateful for in our lives. Sometimes we desire to have more but are incapable of managing the things we have right now. If you are grateful and responsible for what you have, more opportunities are sure to come.

This next statement may sound a little awkward or unusual, but there is something that I have done in the past when interviewing someone for a job that gives me some insight into who they are and if they would be a good fit for the position. I would try to get a look at the person's car. It might be as easy as, "Hey, let's continue this conversation over lunch. Can you drive?" Or I might take a break and walk into the parking lot to look at their mode of transportation. Now don't jump to conclusions and let me explain. I wasn't looking to see what kind of car they drove or how nice it was; I wanted to know if they took care of it, regardless of its age or value. Was the inside of it a disaster zone? This reveals more than you think, especially if this person is being considered for their organization or administrative skills. You don't really see the real individual in an interview, but if I could see how you live, how you treat others in secret, your closet, your bathroom, or anything that is yours, it would give me a glimpse, a more in-depth look into who you are and your level of gratitude. When we first meet someone, we aren't meeting the real person. We get the imposter, the charlatan, or the fake self.

I've been around people who are financially struggling and live modestly but value and take care of the things they have. I've also been in some upscale homes that looked like a slum in the poorest third world county. I'll never forget visiting a village in Mozambique, Africa. I was caught off guard as I watched this young lady raking the dirt floor of her home to prepare for us to be her guest. A thatched shack was all she had, and it was unbelievably clean and cared for. I knew how to act in that place. This may seem a little superficial or even judgmental, but I can assure you it reveals something of the condition of the soul and your appreciation for where you are and what you have right now.

I recently started binge-watching a reality show called *Million Dollar Listing Los Angeles*. I love houses, and Los Angeles has some of the coolest, most eccentric homes anywhere. Do you know what I have never seen during one of their open houses or viewings? A trashed or dirty home. Why is that? How you care for yourself and the things you have communicates something about your level of gratitude. Stop focusing on what you don't have and care for what you have been given. Prove yourself worthy of where you are and what you have been entrusted with, and the next steps will come naturally.

"The worst lies are the lies we tell ourselves."
- Richard Bach

Tip the scale in your favor. I don't believe in balance. If you are on the fence, you are leaning one way or the other. You didn't burn and consume precisely 2,000 calories today. Don't fool yourself. Life is not a zero-sum game. At the end of the day, you either worked too much, loved too little, burned more than you consumed, consumed more than you burned, spent more than made, or made more than you spent. Life is about making sacrifices for the things you value and want, leaning to one side of that fence more than the other, and recognizing you will have victories and losses every day. Someone will win, and someone will lose. You will have to decide what sacrifices you are willing to make for the things you want or want to change, but don't fool yourself with this notion that balance actually exists. You either succeeded and moved closer to your goals today, or you lost ground and drifted further away.

*"How you make others feel about
themselves says a lot about you."*
- Unknown

    I'm not an encourager by nature. I don't know why, and that bothers me. It's a simple gesture that can not only change someone's day; it can alter the course of their life.

    Words are powerful. They can cut to the bone or make you believe you can fly. They have a lasting impact. You are probably still holding on to words of pain that someone vomited on you. They don't go away quickly, but you also have those lasting words of inspiration that you will always carry and let carry you. I came to believe that I don't encourage because I don't need encouragement, but that just isn't so. Observing someone who fully accepts my praise and truth makes me feel good. It makes me feel useful. Receiving words of encouragement, especially from someone I value, and respect ignites my soul and gives me the boldness to move into places I may have never ventured without them. Unfortunately, even as I write this, encouraging others is unnatural for me and something I have to work on and consciously think about in the moment. Test this today. Intentionally make an effort to encourage someone and witness the effect it has on them. The impact and power of your words might surprise you.

"Never ruin an apology with an excuse."
- Benjamin Franklin

Own your mistakes. When you are wrong, admit it. There is something powerful with a person who can take responsibility when they make a mistake. Unfortunately, our default is to defend and explain ourselves when we are exposed or at fault. Psychologists call our initial reaction to a fearful situation the Fight or Flight response, but I think we should add "defend" to this philosophy. It seems to be the initial reaction for most people when they are confronted with a mistake. I have had bosses and family members (no names) who would never admit they were wrong and were utterly unaware of the respect they would have gained by just saying, "I'm sorry," "my bad," "I messed up." It requires letting your guard down and allowing yourself to be vulnerable. Brene Brown describes vulnerability as our greatest measure of courage. If you want to dive deeper into the power of vulnerability, pick up one of her books. This is where I learned how powerful it could be to allow yourself to be exposed. Vulnerability is vital if you are in a position of leadership.

Most of the leaders I have been around wouldn't find their first traits listed as vulnerability or humility. Fear and intimidation seem to be the norm. Most follow Niccolo Machiavelli's philosophy of "I'd rather be feared than loved." Not much vulnerability or humility going on there. Sure, it works if you want a quick response. Parents use this method of power and control with their children all the time to get them to do what they want. The problem is, it doesn't last and ultimately damages the relationship. Meanwhile, humble, vulnerable, and empathetic individuals will often emerge as the most powerful and probably the most loved among their peers and relationships. People will give their life for someone they love and respect. I can't think of a more enduring quality than a leader who owns their faults and is willing to share them openly. People who lead by fear will experience a revolving door of minions who only tolerate them for a short time. Try it sometime. "I'm sorry." "I made a mistake." "Please forgive me." "I value our relationship." This practice sounds easy, but it can be extremely tough. Still, I believe the outcome will utterly surprise you.

"I've never viewed myself as particularly talented. Where I excel is ridiculous, sickening work ethic. You know, while the other guy's sleeping, I'm working."
- Will Smith

I'll admit, I used to see people who were rich and powerful as pretentious and entitled. It must be nice to have someone drive you around, clean your home, take care of the yard, cook your meals. I wish I were that privileged and lucky. Over time with a little life experience and maturity, I came to realize that most of these people didn't aspire to accomplish their goals with the objective of gaining wealth and influence so they could have a comfortable life. They were driven by a fueled passion and determined to let nothing stop them from reaching their objective. People of influence are often some of the hardest workers around. How foolish it would be for them to spend their time doing menial tasks when they are gifted at producing jobs, starting companies, leading, creating beauty, inspiring people, changing the world for the better. I wouldn't expect Mark Cuban to mow his grass or clean his toilets, but I bet he would if he had to.

Some of the most recognized people we know reached their goals because of a ridiculous, sickening work ethic. Venus and Serena Williams were so committed to their craft that they were hitting balls at 6:00 a.m. by the time they were seven & eight years old. Yahoo CEO Marissa Mayer routinely put in 130-hour work weeks while she was at Google. Sometimes she slept under her desk. Kobe Bryant was known for his insane work ethic throughout his career. When he was a rookie, he would shoot balls in the gym when the lights were out. Even after achieving success, Mark Wahlberg's still has an outrageous daily routine that starts at 2:30 a.m. Most of us desire the fruits of success with little understanding or appreciation of how hard it is to get there. Next time you see someone hop into a limo, helicopter, or private jet, don't assume they have it easy and the world is their oyster. Their work ethic might surprise you, and there's often a price to pay for that. Many successful people are work alcoholics with disastrous home lives, but victory isn't without sacrifice. I'm not advocating 130-hour work weeks, but if you want something bad enough, nothing can get in the way. Just be careful that the things that do get in the way aren't more valuable than the desired goal.

"Juicy fruit is gonna move ya,
It chews so soft, it gets right to ya.
The taste, the taste, the taste,
Is gonna move ya."
- *1980's Juicy Fruit Commercial*

In the military, I worked in aviation. One day we needed to get one of the aircraft brought into the hangar for some maintenance. I went into the appropriate department and asked one of the technicians I knew if they could bring number seven into the hangar.

He looked at me and said, "Juicy Fruit."

I knew these guys were busy and had a lot to do, but I didn't understand his response. I asked again, and he said, "Juicy Fruit." No matter what I said, his response was the same.

I was starting to get pissed. "What the hell are you talking about?"

He finally broke and started laughing. He explained that whenever he became frustrated and overwhelmed with people, he gave them the same answer, "Juicy Fruit." Yes, it is childish and silly but his way of not letting things get to him or, as he would say, "I don't allow everyone to rent space in my head."

Admittedly, and I understand this is immature and unprofessional, I have used this several times since. Mostly with someone I was irritated with just to piss them off, but that's not my point. My emphasis is that words are powerful, and the words you allow to aggravate you now have power over you.

Have you ever lingered for days about someone's comments about you? You have just let this person's words have control over your life, and they are probably the last person you want to have in your head. I witnessed this daily while working with troubled teens. My family worked and lived with these kids for three years. Words, especially among teenage girls, were extremely potent. Yes, we had a home of adolescent girls: a little place I like to refer to as Estrogen Hell. As Colonel Walter Kurtz said, "the horror.... the horror" (you might have to look that one up). I regress. These girls had learned early on that their words had power. The power to build up or the ability to tear down, and the exceptionally devious ones could use their words to invoke a physical response from another girl, which would surely end in her demise.

This exchange happens every day in society. A few choice words are exchanged, and the first one to make it physical and throw a punch is going to jail. We had two girls who hated each other, but only one of them understood the impact of her words. She was a vernacular wizard and could get under anyone's skin. These two frequently went at it, and the first girl to make it physical and attack, lost. Then one day, I saw the most incredible transformation happen. Our counselor was working with these two girls, and he told the one who would lose these verbal battles that she should bow down and worship the other girl, not the response anyone was expecting. At that moment, she realized how much power she had been giving up to her adversary. She finally understood that these were just words, and she had given this girl complete control over her emotions. With her newfound revelation, she no longer allowed anyone to rent space in her head. She also had a little help from her House Dad, who armed her with two words whenever she became overwhelmed: "Juicy Fruit."

*"Don't believe everything you hear
and only half of what you see."*
- Unknown

Zig Ziglar tells a story of a time when he won a prized ham for a sales contest. He brought the ham home and gave it to his wife, who quickly cut off the end of the ham and put it in the pan.

He asked his wife, "Why did you cut off the end of the ham?"

She said that was how she had always cooked a ham. She learned it from her mother.

"But why?" he asked.

They called his wife's mother and asked her the same question. She said I did it that way because that's the way my mother did it. Now curiosity had the best of them. They called granny. When they asked her why she cut off the end of the ham before she cooked it, she said, "I don't know why you are doing it, but my pan was too short."

It's incredible the things we believe that simply aren't true. No, toilets don't flush counterclockwise in Australia; you can't see the Great Wall of China from space; most people do use 100% of their brain; Einstein was a good student in school; sitting too close to the TV won't ruin your eyesight; there's no dye in pools that shows up when you pee in it (pee away); coffee won't stunt your growth; you can't get warts from a frog; Santa's not watching; and many more.

You may not like to hear this, but poverty often produces poverty, wealth creates wealth, prejudice breeds prejudice. We are often products of our environment and upbringing without questioning why. Religion is a big one. So many Catholics, Muslims, Christians, Buddhists, Hindus, etc. that I have encountered have no idea why they have given their lives to this belief. They follow this life-altering spiritual journey because of what they were told or taught. Few have explored the facts and decided for themselves, yet so many continue through the motions of something they have never really questioned or tested. That's a big commitment for something you have given your forever to. Ask questions, lots of them. Seek answers for yourself. You will never wholly believe or fully commit to anything without exploring or experiencing it personally.

*"It is not happy people who are thankful.
It is thankful people who are happy."*
- Unknown

    I can't think of a better way to start a day than overtly or silently cataloging the things I am thankful for in my life. I have heard that some people will take pictures of the things they are grateful for or appreciate. They keep a catalog of photos that remind them of gratitude. It has been proven that thankful people are healthier, happier, more confident, and better sleepers than those who aren't. Is your glass of life half-full or half-empty? Are you focused on what you don't have or grateful for what you have been given? This sets the tone for your entire day. Expressing kindness or gratitude floods your brain with dopamine, giving you a natural high. Take this a step further and tell someone you are thankful for them. Pass the baton of thankfulness to someone else. Receiving appreciation is inspiring and powerful. You could change the trajectory of their entire day, week, or life by a few simple words spoken or written just for them.

"A man's got to know his limitations."
- Dirty Harry

I ran track in middle and high school. I wasn't great at it, but I had two events that I excelled in: the pole vault and the 220-yard dash. I learned rather quickly that I wasn't a distance runner. I didn't have the patience or stamina for it. Anything over 220 yards was a challenge. While traveling for a track meet, the coach needed someone to run the 440. He asked me; actually, he told me that I would fill the spot because our team was required to have someone participate in this event. To no avail, I tried to convince him I had never run the 440 and that I was the wrong choice, but my words fell on deaf ears. The next thing I knew, I was in the starting block, and the gun went off.

When you are running the 220, it's an all-out sprint, and that's how I started this race. By the time we hit the 220 mark, I was leading this race by a considerable margin. I had this quick thought that maybe I should have been running this event all along. The coach must have seen something in me. Perhaps he was right. At about 230 yards, my legs decided to stop, well, not completely, just switch to jog mode. I didn't know what to do. My mind was saying "go," but my legs just wouldn't, and I started to see everyone, and I mean everyone, pass me. Now, if you know anything about track, you would remember the last 100 yards are finished in front of the stands, and I was now about 50 yards behind everyone. I jogged the final 100 yards listening to the fans, and my teammates try their best to encourage me to finish. Did I mention this was 9th grade? If you remember anything from middle school, you can empathize with this moment of sheer humiliation. Unfortunately, the day wasn't finished; as the team got on the bus to go home, someone gave me an orange soda to drink. I was so thirsty I chugged it down, and once that bus started moving, it came straight out of me, and we all enjoyed the long ride back to school with orange soda hurled all over the floor. Thankfully we didn't have internet or cell phones back then. It would have made a great video on social media, but it didn't matter; word travels fast in middle school. Needless to say, the coach never again asked anyone to run a race that they hadn't trained for ahead of time.

There have been so many times in life that I wanted things I wasn't ready or prepared to handle. I have served under many leaders whose positions I wanted just because I thought I could do it better. If I only had more money. More influence. More responsibility. More opportunity. *Why did they make that decision? I wouldn't have done it that way.* Sometimes it's a blessing when you don't get the things you want. Ever heard the

Garth Brooks song, "Unanswered Prayers?" It takes some maturity and life experience to realize that had you been empowered with that coveted position, you would have failed miserably because you weren't ready for it. Be careful what you ask for. Influence exceeding character is a recipe for disaster.

Sex, Religion, & Politics

Everything I know and you should, too...

"If you can learn a simple trick, Scout, you'll get along a lot better with all kinds of folks.
You never really understand a person until you consider things from his point of view until you climb inside of his skin and walk around in it."
- Atticus Finch, To Kill A Mockingbird

Sometimes I just don't understand people.

Why are you driving so slow in the left lane? The left lane is where the fast drivers are. Can't you see I'm in a hurry?

Are you always late?

Are you seriously going to step in front of me in this line? Who do you think you are?

I was talking. Stop interrupting me.

If you start a sentence with "no offense," I'm already offended.

No, I don't want to hear your phone conversation.

Can you control your kids? I've raised mine and shouldn't have to deal with yours.

What do you mean you aren't ready to order? We've been standing in line for 20 minutes.

Your car has a turn signal for a reason.

Can you eat that with your mouth closed?

Okay, I'll admit these are mostly first world problems but some of the things that drive me looney. Have you ever had someone block you in the left lane only to realize they were there to make a left turn? I was so frustrated following someone who was driving ridiculously slow, and as I followed them into the gas station, I realized they cruised in on fumes and were nearly out of gas. Then I watched them put $3 of gas in their car because they were broke. I felt terrible after that display of judgment. What if that person you are irritated with is doing the best they can at the moment? You just don't know how someone was raised, what they have experienced, or why they do the things they do if you haven't walked in their shoes. Think of your favorite restaurant. Most of my favorite places to eat are the most expensive. My favorite place to eat in all the world is the Green Valley Restaurant. Unfortunately, the Green Valley Restaurant is located in Jericho. That's Jericho in the West Bank near Jerusalem. I've been privileged to eat there several times, and they have some of the freshest, most amazing food I have ever had.

Now think about who the best Bail Bond company is in your town. Where do you go to get the best deal when someone in the family is arrested? Okay, how about the fairest Title Loan company? Who will give you the best arrangement and treat you fairly when you need some cash and all you have for collateral is your car? Can't think of one? Could it be that this just isn't part of your lifestyle?

There are people who can tell you who the best Bail Bondsman is in town because that's the world they live in or have been exposed to most of their lives. Without putting yourself in their shoes and seeing through their lenses, you can't fully understand why someone makes the choices they make. I sometimes try to create possible motives in my head when I see someone making choices I just don't understand. This is a helpful exercise, and it momentarily puts me in their shoes, but there are times when you have to call it like it is. It's not acceptable, nor is it an excuse to disrespect, intimidate, dishonor, or hurt someone because that's the way you were raised. That might be the world you were subjected to and influenced by, but the actions don't justify the means. We see people through the lenses of our life, not theirs. Perspective matters.

There is a question. It could be the most difficult question and also the most helpful. It is a question I wish I would have asked more often. Admittedly, I have probably only asked it twice in my entire life. If you genuinely want to know more about yourself and make some necessary changes in your life, this is the best question you can ask. Sit down with someone who knows you and ask them this: "What do I need to work on?"

Ouch!! I hate this question. Tell me what I'm good at. Tell me what you like about me, but don't tell me what's wrong. I want encouragement, not negativity or judgment. Few people have the courage to ask this question. Unconsciously, you probably already know the answer. I knew it before the other person ever opened their mouth, but it was so helpful to hear them say it.

Hearing the words out loud was difficult but freeing. It confirmed what I had already suspected. Let me be clear. You aren't necessarily looking for someone who will give you a soft, gentle, reserved answer. The person you ask needs to know you, but they don't need to like you. I promise you this, by the time that conversation is finished, you will have broadened your relationship with this person, whether you intended to or not, and received some vital feedback to help you going forward. Can you handle the truth?

"Come away, O human child!
To the waters and the wild
With a faery, hand in hand,
For the world's more full of weeping
Than you can understand."
- William Butler Yeats

As a parent, I envied and longed for my children's purity and innocence when they were little. They believed in everything, and it reminded me of how freeing it was to be a child. I remember the first time I saw a crack in their armor and how it changed their perspective on the world. I sat them down and told them I had not been truthful about old Saint Nicholas. There was no Santa Claus. They took the news well, but I could see the disappointment and loss in their eyes. As time went on, the reality of the world crept in and robbed them of their belief system. As a parent, you know it's coming and hate seeing your children experience disappointment and hurt. The innocence fades, and they seek out who they will be in this world. As they search for their purpose, I want them to know this is not a journey they will have to take alone.

At the end of the movie *Superman Returns*, there is a scene that just filleted me when I saw it. I had to sit in the theater and pull myself together before I could leave. It is almost as bad as the end of Saving Private Ryan when Ryan asks his wife if he has lived a good life and if he's a good man. You're not human if that doesn't wreck you. In this film, Superman has just found out that he is Jason's father. He flies into Jason's room while he is sleeping and speaks these words over him. *"You will be different, sometimes you'll feel like an outcast, but you'll never be alone. You will make my strength your own. You will see my life through your eyes, as your life will be seen through mine."* When you read that, who's voice do you hear? Who speaks this over you? A mother or father? God? A family member? A close friend? I hope my children hear my voice. I hope they know I will always be here. That my strength will be theirs as I witness their lives through my eyes.

The fallible father.

Oh, and one last piece of advice from the famous Will Rogers: "Never miss a good chance to shut up."

Notes

Page 6
"MONEY" Words and Music by Roger Waters
TRO - (c) Copyright 1973 (Renewed) Hampshire House Publishing
Corp., New York, New York
International Copyright Secured Made in U.S.A.
All Rights Reserved Including Public Performance For Profit
Used by Permission

Page 26
Scary Close by Donald Miller (www.storybrand.com) – used with
permission

Page 27
"I Want To Know What Love Is" - Michael Jones/Somerset Songs
Publishing, Inc. – used with permission